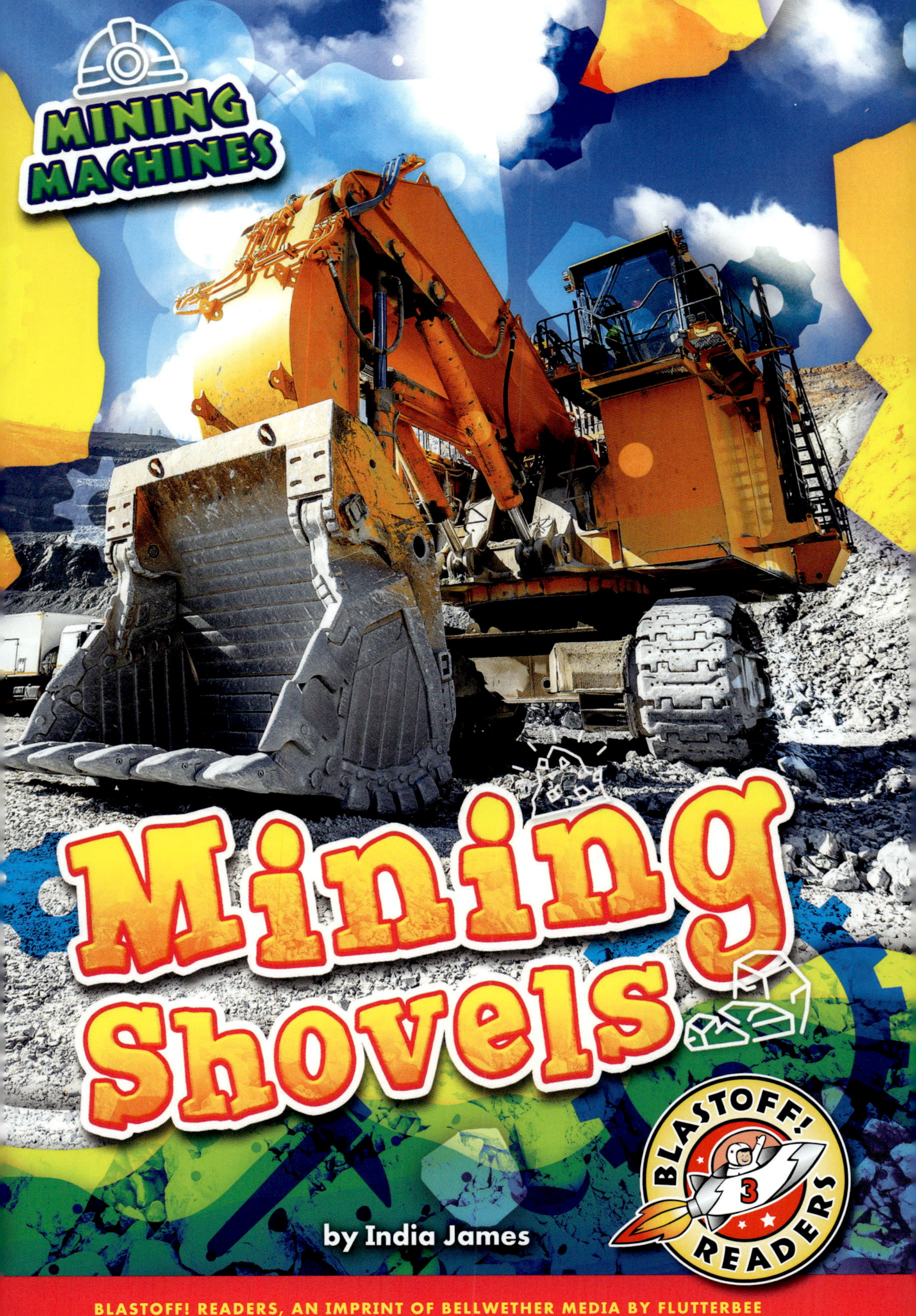

Mining Shovels

by India James

BLASTOFF! READERS, AN IMPRINT OF BELLWETHER MEDIA BY FLUTTERBEE

Blastoff! Readers are carefully developed by literacy experts to build reading stamina and move students toward fluency by combining standards-based content with developmentally appropriate text.

Level 1 provides the most support through repetition of high-frequency words, light text, predictable sentence patterns, and strong visual support.

Level 2 offers early readers a bit more challenge through varied sentences, increased text load, and text-supportive special features.

Level 3 advances early-fluent readers toward fluency through increased text load, less reliance on photos, advancing concepts, longer sentences, and more complex special features.

★ **Blastoff! Universe**

Reading Level

Grade K

Grades 1–3

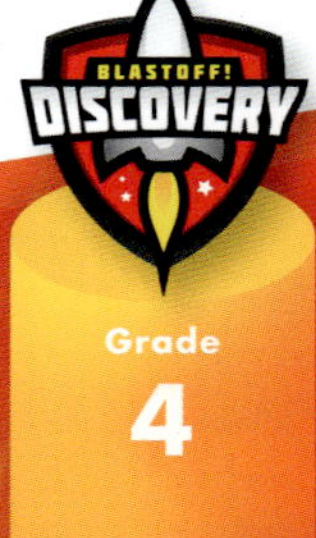

Grade 4

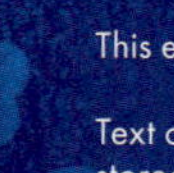

This edition first published in 2027 by Bellwether Media, Inc.

For information regarding permission, write to Bellwether Media, Inc., Attention: Permissions Department, 3500 American Blvd W, Suite 150, Bloomington, MN 55431.

Library of Congress Cataloging-in-Publication Data is available at www.loc.gov or upon request from the publisher.

ISBN: 9798898800710 (hardcover)
ISBN: 9798898801953 (ebook)

Editor: Kieran Downs Designer: Jeffrey Kollock

Printed in the United States of America, North Mankato, MN.

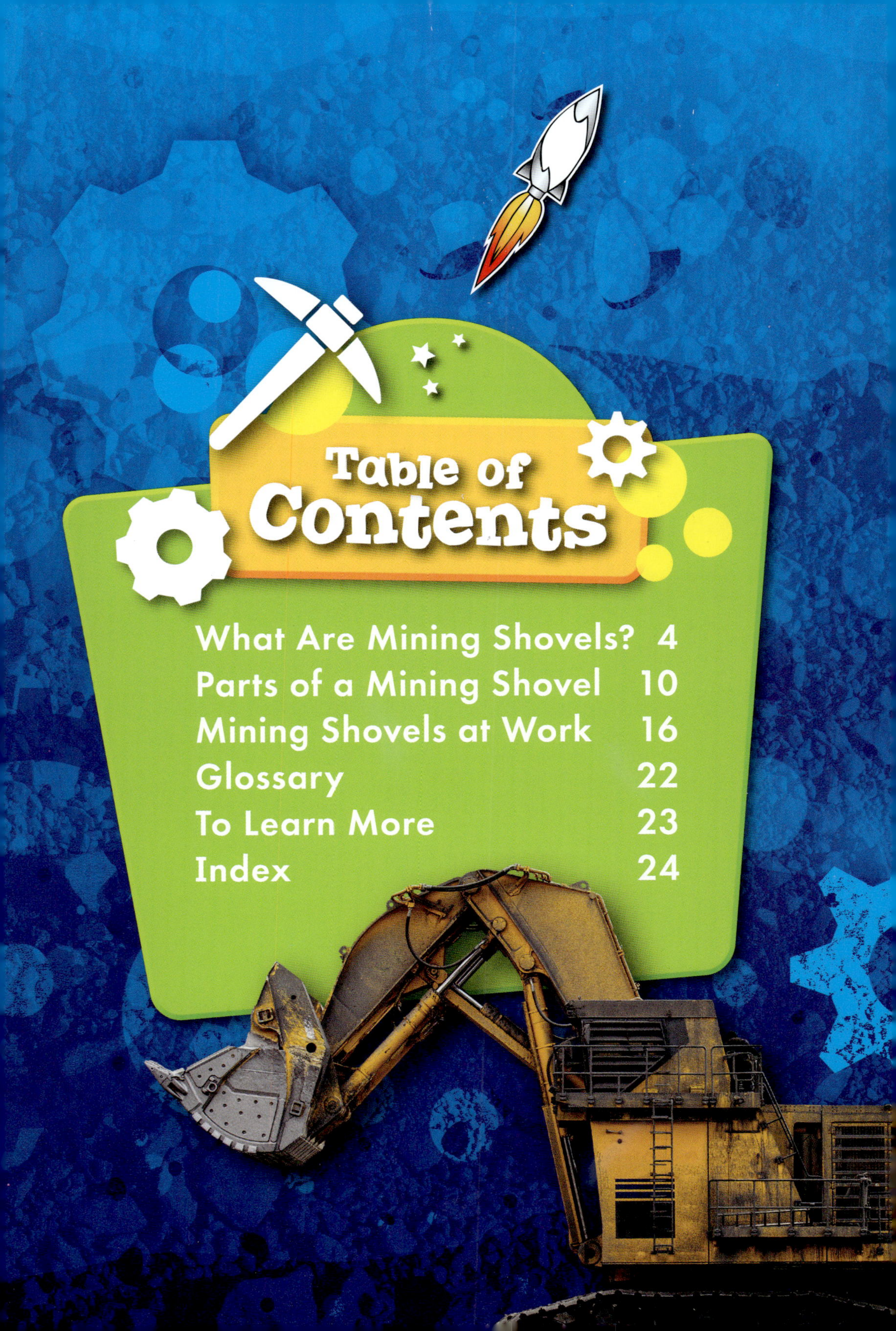

Table of Contents

What Are Mining Shovels?

ore

Mining shovels are big machines. They are used to scoop a lot of **material** at one time. They lift dirt, **coal**, and **ore**.

Big buckets help mining shovels do their job.

Mining shovels are used in mines in many different ways. They move dirt in **surface mines** and **strip mines**.

They help find coal and other materials.

Mining shovels come in many sizes. They often weigh more than 300 tons (272 metric tons). The largest can weigh over 1,000 tons (907 metric tons).

The machines are often powered by **diesel fuel**.

diesel fuel

Parts of a Mining Shovel

A giant bucket is at the front of a mining shovel. The bucket scoops up material from the ground.

The bucket faces away from the mining shovel. The arm connects to the bucket.

A long **boom** connects the arm to the **cab**. The boom moves the bucket into position.

Hydraulics move the bucket, arm, and boom.

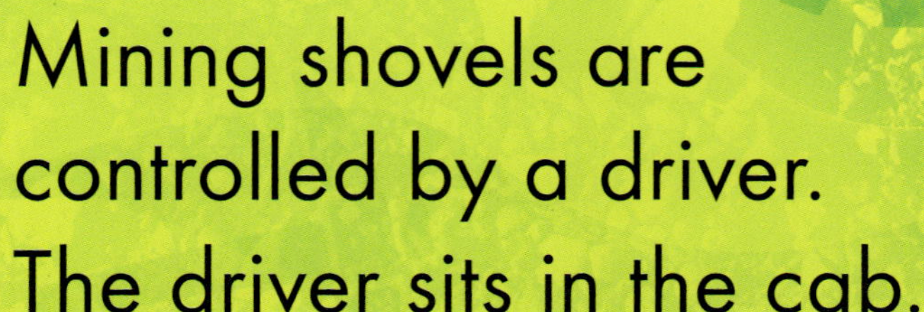

Mining shovels are controlled by a driver. The driver sits in the cab.

Mining Shovel Parts

boom

arm

cab

bucket

tracks

Mining shovels move to different places in mines. **Tracks** let mining shovels move on rough ground.

Mining Shovels at Work

Mining shovels dig up large amounts of material. They scoop up dirt, rock, and ore with their buckets.

They move the materials away from where they dug it up.

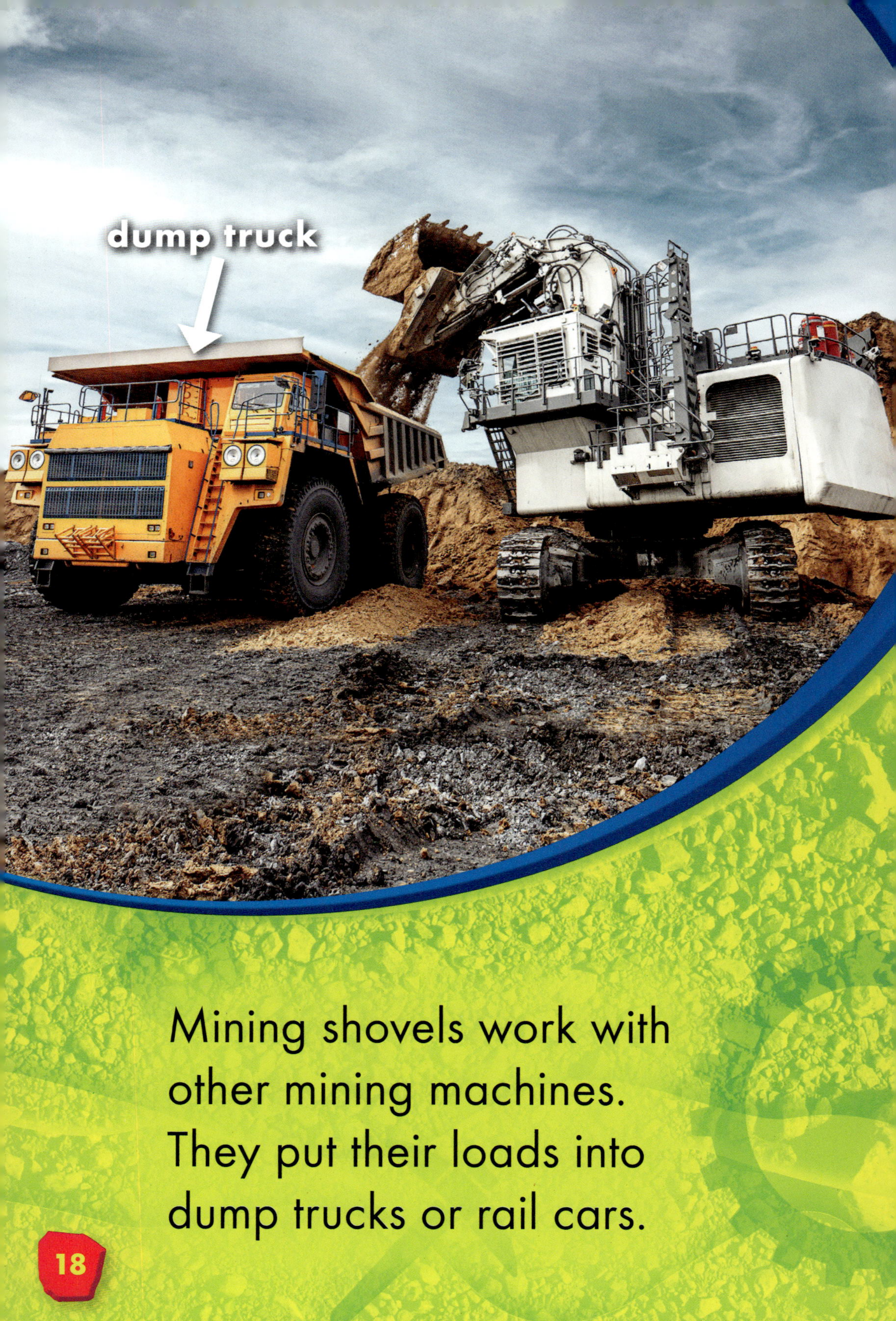

Mining shovels work with other mining machines. They put their loads into dump trucks or rail cars.

The material is taken away from the mine. It is put to use in many ways.

Mining shovels are expensive to build. Each one has a different size, shape, and power.

Mining Shovel Profile

Caterpillar 6030

weighs 324 tons (294 metric tons)

can lift 21.6 cubic yards (16.5 cubic meters) of dirt in one scoop

driver sits 21.3 feet (6.5 meters) above the ground

They are created to be perfect for each project. Mining shovels get the job done!

Glossary

boom—a long arm on a mining shovel

cab—the part of a mining shovel where the driver sits

coal—a hard black substance that is burned for fuel

diesel fuel—a type of oil that is burned in diesel engines

hydraulics—systems that make parts move by forcing fluids through small holes

material—things that are used to help make something else

ore—a valuable material that occurs naturally in the earth

strip mines—mines that dig up materials from shallow strips in the ground

surface mines—mines that get materials from dirt near Earth's surface

tracks—moving parts of a machine that touch the ground

To Learn More

AT THE LIBRARY

James, India. *Bucket-Wheel Excavators.* Minneapolis, Minn.: Bellwether Media, 2027.

James, Ryan. *Excavators.* New York, N.Y.: Crabtree Publishing, 2025.

Rogers, Marie. *Huge Earthmovers.* New York, N.Y.: PowerKids Press, 2022.

ON THE WEB

FACTSURFER

Factsurfer.com gives you a safe, fun way to find more information.

1. Go to www.factsurfer.com.

2. Enter "mining shovels" into the search box and click 🔍.

3. Select your book cover to see a list of related content.

Index

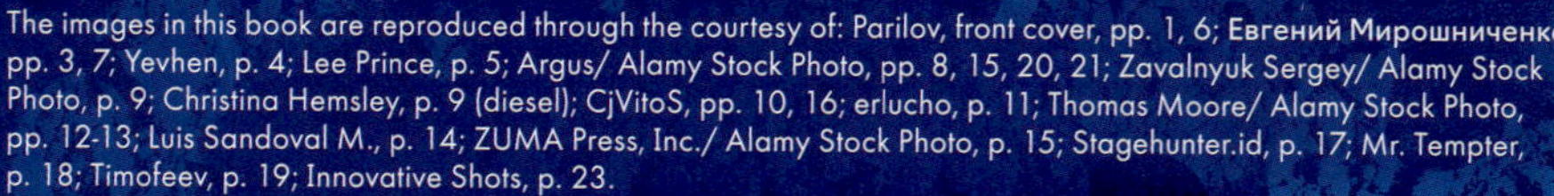

The images in this book are reproduced through the courtesy of: Parilov, front cover, pp. 1, 6; Евгений Мирошниченко pp. 3, 7; Yevhen, p. 4; Lee Prince, p. 5; Argus/ Alamy Stock Photo, pp. 8, 15, 20, 21; Zavalnyuk Sergey/ Alamy Stock Photo, p. 9; Christina Hemsley, p. 9 (diesel); CjVitoS, pp. 10, 16; erlucho, p. 11; Thomas Moore/ Alamy Stock Photo, pp. 12-13; Luis Sandoval M., p. 14; ZUMA Press, Inc./ Alamy Stock Photo, p. 15; Stagehunter.id, p. 17; Mr. Tempter, p. 18; Timofeev, p. 19; Innovative Shots, p. 23.